West Virginians

Trent Busch

Cyberwit.net
HIG 45 Kaushambi Kunj, Kalindipuram
Allahabad - 211011 (U.P.) India
http://www.cyberwit.net
Tel: +(91) 9415091004
E-mail: info@cyberwit.net

Printed at Repro India Limited.

To Carol, Laura, and Bret

AUTHOR'S NOTE

Though I lived the first twenty-one years of my life in West Virginia, I, like most of us in the early years of our lives, was not aware of or thought much about my family, the people, their customs, the small towns, the bigger cities, or the state itself. I knew absolutely nothing about West Virginia politics. Only after I started writing poetry did I find out what I knew. I guess I have written in excess of a thousand poems, and I have discovered that at least three-fourths of them started out with some fragment from those first twenty-one years. The fifty plus years since then seem much shorter and less influential in my memory than the first twenty-one. Those twenty-one years dominate these poems not necessarily in time but through some image or sound or smell that was evoked in the proximity of whatever room, carrell, or office (and on whatever desk or typewriter) I was attending at the time.

There is, of course, much of me in every one of these West Virginians, just as there is much of me in the mountains, hills, rivers, towns, and roads that slip in as background. Not every one of them has liquor on their breath, but each one has some moment of light that arouses some joyful color or trembling shadow in the corner of their minds, which, I feel, helps them know where they came from and who they are.

Trent Busch

I would especially like to thank Faye Echols for her breathtaking art, from the first drawing she did for me of William Faulkner more than fifty years ago to the three covers she has offered for my books of poems.

James Carper as well deserves much praise for his ability to capture in a photograph an ordinary man and present him on the page with dignity.

Acknowledgements

Thanks to the editors of the following publications where poems, sometimes with different titles and in different form, first appeared:

Agni Online, "The Forties"
American Literary Review, "Night Drama"
Anthology of Magazine Verse and Yearbook of Poetry, 1985, "Staying"
Antietam Review, "Family History"
artisan, "Miles Later"
Arts and Letters, "Curt's Girl" and "Kick the Tire"
Atlanta Review, "Pleasant Hill School"
The Broome Review, "Nomenclature"
Calamaro Magazine, "Courting, 1945"
The California Quarterly, "The Alleghenies"
Carolina Quarterly, "Romey Davis"
Clackamas Literary Review, "Grandmother"
The Distillery, "Winter in Mount Storm"
Dominion Review, "Nameless"
Epiphany, "The Kanawha" and "The Other Place"
The Florida Review, "Back Road to Charleston"
The Gamut, "Left"
Greensboro Review, "Treading Time"
Guesthouse, "Joe and the Water Main" and "Joe and Uncle Jesse"
Hubbub, "Chasing Women"
The Hudson Review, "Near Beckley"
Interim, "Pupils of Discipline"
Into the Teeth of the Wind, "The Pink Whorehouse"
The Kennesaw Review, "Out of Work in Parkersburg"
The Laurel Review, "A Note in a Voice"

Mankato Poetry Review, "The Garden"
Manoa, "The Sweetness of Frenzy"
The Marlboro Review, "Three Sons"
The Moving Force Journal, "But Its Own"
The New Criterion, "Spencer High School"
New England Review, "The Country"
Nimrod, "Mr Stevens"
North Dakota Review, "They Made the Best Red Whiskey in Wirt County"
Oxford Magazine, "Mona Richards, Rt. 4"
Passager Journal, "Fridays Far Away as Heaven"
Permafrost Magazine, "Sonata"
The Poet's Page, "Sandra Schroeder, Bride"
Poetry, "Gay" and "Staying"
Prairie Winds, "The Workman"
Puckerbrush Review, "Straight Creek"
Rattle, "Dark Coats" and "Smittys"
The Ravens Perch, "Direction by the Compass"
Riverwind, "Coal Fork"
The Roanoke Review, "Coming from There" and "Smoke"
Salt Hill, "1949"
Small Pond Magazine, "Country Church"
The Snail's Pace, "Le Breun the History Teacher"
Sou'wester, "West Virginia Oil"
Stone Country, "Round Rock Creek"
The Tampa Review, "Sure Tones"
Terminus, "The Dumpsters"
Thin Air Magazine, "Aunt Phyllis"
Third Wednesday, "On Reading a Poem by . . ."
Trajectory, "Letter: An Ode"
Water-Stone Review, "Ancestral"
Whetstone, "Macfarlan Bridge"
White Pelican Review, "Hughes River"

WEST VIRGINIA

Everyone has a place
they like to think as theirs,
whether state or city
or just some simple ridge
that offered a shoulder once,

and though photographed,
surveyed, and walked on,
remains, its stance against
the sky, if not the same,
as permanent as the sun.

Here today, as we can,
we offer you our arms
to be held as a teacher
at year's end holds all
her pupils as one child.

Old friend, we care nothing
about your history, what
you did in the war, how
much oil and coal were
taken from your belly,

or who your governors
have been and, as we would
be forgiven, forgive
whatever you did to
deserve your bastard name.

Though we have gone away,
the wind will shake again
your leaves this summer,
winter snowflakes will fall,
and while we live on earth

you will steal behind the backs
of all your sons and daughters,
evoking their peculiar
memories, singling out those
ridges and hills you left behind.

CONTENTS

1. THE FORTIES

THE ALLEGHENIES

The tracks
led into the thicket,
a dark hole
in the vines
and briars.

The snow
was falling harder.
The boy turned
to see
his own steps
whitening
behind him.

All day,
up mountains,
across ridges,
he had followed
the foreign tracks
of this animal,
a hand wide,
three-sided—
now this thicket.

Sometimes boys
wander too far
into the Alleghenies
in winter.

When they return
parents and neighbors
do not know them:
they look too wise
for their years
and have turned into
little, wizened men.

Parents lock their doors
against them
and let the smoke
from their stoves
drift against the sky.

The boys
turn wild and cry
in the mountains;
in their loneliness
they make three-sided
tracks in the snow.

LEFT

We cross the ridge's back.
We travel west,
right hemisphere
in control.

It is a bloody trip,
full of dragon teeth
and eyes in trees,
mapped illogically
and filled with fear:

low cave with
a hundred ready
snakes, darkening
sky behind us,

astonished girl
whose naked breast
is smeared
for sacrifice,

awakened face
falling from a bed
built in branches.

And the ridge itself
alien, trying
to topple us
into right-handedness.

But we travel west,
sinister left
leading to the valley
of serpents
and certain evil,

unchained, wrong-headed,
making our awkward
and primitive way
past the flaming swords
protecting Eden.

THE FORTIES

In small towns in the forties
cats did not indulge mice;
they entertained themselves,

and Bill Snider drove his
dad's green Buick out dirt
roads, dusting the peach trees.

There were the usual dry
vines spit from anxious mouths
while the wild hay tasseled.

At stores, while supper fried,
white sacks flowered and hands
slapped their knees by dusk light.

Porcelain chinked as heat
blew the curtains, and mud
sucked the water from snow.

Outside, inside, these were
the small presents that kept
the lean and hungry hard

for the nothing past daylight
that would soften and ripen
and explode on the young.

COURTING, 1945

The morning she had been
looking for anyone
to write to, she picked him,
balling a half dozen
pieces of paper into
a small woven basket
before she chose one,
right words for his calling,
"My stairs must be redone."

Of course, unsuspecting,
he had a million things
to do, then get over . . . .
Though his carpentry
did not last forever,
she did, or so it seemed
seven childbirths after,
she closing up to men as
he quit wanting women.

Bending in a chair tying
his shoes the morning she
died, he told this story,
searching for anyone
to listen, yet choosing
her whom he most hated,
crying a life's wrath down
upon her, not eased the way
he felt he would be eased.

MILES LATER

The old man holds his chair,
a blanket covering
his knees, staring into
what none of us can say

as we move around him
as we would move around
a stone, blue cap over
a face no longer shaved.

Miles later, after this
day, birthday he could not
foresee, and never saw,
music he did not hear,

we can watch the brown hands
that threaded hooks for us,
that righted wagons, set
up bottles along beams,

the love and anger in eyes
that seeing birth and death
defied love and anger,
the voice as sane as God's.

We cannot right him now;
only later can we
say here was a man who
lived his life on barter:

first, nose against the sky,
now scolded to a corner.
We can say then that old
age was never for sale.

THREE SONS

I
Sun gleams off the tombstones
on the ridge, May sunny
morning and the smooth to
touch gray marble gleaming
and all inscriptions clear.

The crow over the ridge
flying, bright sun gleaming
off his hard wings, calling,
his cry muffled as he
sails down the deep hollow.

II
Where feet pass on the wooden floor
voices are low, talk in the hall
low, someone elbowing the door,
careful, not letting the wood fall.

In the kitchen women in Greek
chorus, dressed in shawls, tell a ride
said first by Lorca, wash the cheek
of both mother and virgin bride.

III
When I was young, I thought
sons lasted forever,
coming in with shirts and
pride torn, capacity
none whatsoever to

understand how when I
reached out my hand I was
waiting only for them
to get wiser, older.

To whom can I give the
impossible answer
when questioned, "What happens
to a mother's heart when
she loses all her sons?"
when I in that instant
see my own powdered face
lying lined and rigid,
them beside me weeping?

IV
They are adding another room
to the house. Workers this morning
with level and square, pine lumber.
They do a good job, and it is
something my husband has wanted.

The money comes from my oldest,
Gerald, who was killed in the war.
Would have been thirty-four today.
Always the dreamiest. Most people
say he looked like his father.

V
Night came and the last boy
was in the ground and I
thought, Dear God, what else have
you planned for this my one
life before it is done.

Her not crying anymore
and the neighbors gone and
when I saw my face in
the window I looked down
but could not see the floor.

VI
The rabbit stretches long before
the fox at dusk, then is caught at
the cemetery gate. Dead, it
is carried gently as a kitten.

The darkened ridge and crows calm as
a house dog barks in the hollow.
Monuments take form, and under
the quick moon cast shadows like men.

DIRECTION BY THE COMPASS

Words reach
but cannot find
the distance,

her voice
clean with answers
as if speaking to
a Sears repairman.

How can summer
apples know
winter wind
in December hollows,

wisp of snow
dancing the line
of crackling
junctures.

Cold, a lighted
phone booth,
naked in the rain.

CURT'S GIRL

A woman of passion surely,
Curt's girl; "I lost my sweetheart,"
he said, his shoulders bird round,
the grief so surprised on his face
it costly resembled a grin.

Rosa, Rosa, standing in the vines,
he her next husband, young
too young, she would wear him thin
fingers said, stopping on a dime
the tractor trailer, her hero.

Curt's girl, high cheekbones, running
her late husband's store too alone;
he second, hauling goods, strong arms,
cooking for his new one, rolling
barrels by night in her store room.

"I lost my sweetheart," forlorn, boom
goes the girl, the sometimes mother
slipping on the slick berm, the worm
urging its sting on the late bloom,
reclaimed by an afternoon wind.

Curt with his girl gone (his lost
sweetheart), ghost truck sloshing on
the creek road stones, the old pain soon,
transferred yonder by rain or moon
to flowers on the pale hillside.

OUT OF WORK IN PARKERSBURG

I set on this
stone wall, a
cigarette between
my fingers.

You want to know
where alone is?

Dress that cost
a hundred dollars.

That's what heaven
is I think,
a girl that just
walloped
your heart.

I don't know why
I picked up this
habit.

Something, maybe,
the poor
do for money.

Mister man,
mister man,
she was lovely.

You want a word,
I'll give you
desperation.

You tell me where
the chance is,
I'll move on.

JOE AND THE WATER MAIN

Goddamnedest piece
of ingenuity I've
ever seen, Joe said,
nodding,

But, Joe, everyone
said, she's raw
concrete hardened.

Can't question you
there, man,
says Joe,

but have you seen
the way that L
comes out of that
T.

But, Joe, you
couldn't chip her
with a pickax.

No, man, no,
but ain't that
the beauty,

take off the collar,
you got the
slickest
threads ever machined,

what a line of joinery!
that, baby, wasn't
made for
no ordinary me.

CHASING WOMEN

A beer between his knees, he slid
the car around turns with one hand,
the steering wheel knob a ruby
gliding in its socket, his hair
damp on the back of his neck.

Oh, we were after *women*, he
eighteen, I two years younger,
talking loud, dazzling
the countryside with speed
and liquor, the moment everything.

So when we asked them to join us,
we were not really struck by their
indifference; we had only time
to ease the needing heart for what
it needed, satisfied we could.

THE PINK WHOREHOUSE

The pink whorehouse in the turn
on Route 53 is
a clot of vines beneath
two dying walnut trees.

The man killed there once with
a small hand .22,
shot twice in the hero chest,
was a man we all knew.

The Saturday nights they
had we drove past, lanterns
in the trees, blue, green, red,
shadows behind the blinds.

Now it's all talk, the steps
leading up the hill (broken
in the middle by the dance)
not even left. I wish

I could tell it and not
exaggerate. I wish.
I wish. I wish I had
some confession to make.

STORE

If my parents died I'd come
and live with her I said,
all the while eyeing the candy
case, the box of balloons open
on the counter, clipped peanuts,

my parents ordering sugar,
flour, cornflakes, salt fish
in a barrel just delivered, how I
was too big in her arms,
her perfume, overprice of rouge.

It was about being her boy when
she told it, her overflowing
heart blowzed out with imagery,
my lowered eyes and quick grin
learned to hide embarrassment.

How strange we surely were
to those outside it, the colors
and smells and listings
combined in that selfishness
for sweetness that united us,

sharing lies with no meanness,
our purses lined at no expense
to others, her husband finding
me the years after she died to
say that he had lost his sweetheart.

PLEASANT HILL SCHOOL

Out the ridge where the small
school used to stand, ruts of
water harbor tadpoles,
prosper beneath the trees.

From the soft breeze playing
in the branches, I try
to hear young voices loud
at tag or soft in watching,

or authoritative words
from our teacher, extolling
Roland's brave commitment
or merits of good spelling.

But I can only try,
for I have seen the ones
who moved to town, city
rounded or sick or dead

from cancer, and the ones
who stayed, gray upon their
heads, their eyes glassy with
age and remembrance.

And if there is singing
in these trees, it is for
the standing ruts filled with
water and bright nights when

the breeze rearranges
shadows, when young emerge
from frozen sleep and fill
the clearing with hoarse song.

PUPILS OF DISCIPLINE

Out a ridge somewhere after the clay
road has forked, a stern man dressed
in a wrinkled shirt sits on a horse
and waits for us to catch up.

He is waiting to descend into
the valley of the other, where
corn has tasseled and now stands in
shocks, where summer has hidden.

Light through the branches of the baring
oaks makes his face a quiet cliff
but we know his impatience, our
speech slight as we hurry after.

Our young lives follow this leader
without contest or challenge, loaning
dissatisfaction for those who
idle in halls of the taken.

He pulls the rein, urges his horse
downward toward that strict valley
where only the damned or pupils
of discipline follow after.

WINTER IN MOUNT STORM

The glint off the barn
roof awakens the owl in
the dead pine halfway
up the mountainside.
He focuses the square hole
in the dark mow, blinks
a dream of running mice.
It is only noon.

In the thicket a hollow
across a fox lifts
its head, listens for hound,
rests nose on paws.

But night, what burning
flash the chickens squawk,
what thumps awaken cattle
in their stalls as light
and shoes go on, shotgun
grabbed from corner
inside the kitchen door.

Any night, this night, halo
around the moon, as winter
thickens, snow begins to fall.

1949

The road is yellow
below the locust trees,
the wind, too, yellow,
bringing a swirling
of cool dust.

No one died, married,
or gave birth;
the sky is like any sky
and no dog howls
throughout the night.

But change that falls
upon a town has fallen,
curling the maple leaves,
holding them
in yellow light.

No one knows what day
it happened, when cars
fell from bridges
and keys broke into
people's houses.

In the mountains they
say there is a letter.
We'll walk as far
as Freed's Store ourselves
if they deliver it.

LE BREUN THE HISTORY TEACHER

If you say we walk
with a stagger and have
moonshine on our breath,
the accent of a teacher
not long out of boots,

you have us right, who can
skin a squirrel in five
minutes flat with a knife
we sharpened ourselves.

When you fought the war
we laid up for winter,
when you passed the act
we let whiskey age
in oak barrels, and when
the vein ran out none
of us took the checks.

Still, your incense lingers,
portraying us not
as artists or young men,
the hornets in your words
far beyond unkindness.

You drew the line
and we stayed out.
You gathered and stormed
to hurt us long enough.
Now we are going on.

2 OLDER THAN THE TREES

THE COUNTRY

The image must fit
the setting:
the hunter jumping
on the brush pile
must wear a red
and black mackinaw
with one button
missing; the rabbit
that breaks
for the fence line
must turn a somersault
when his shotgun
jerks upward
and springs tightly
against his shoulder.

The language must fit
the situation:
the girl who does not
want sex
with the boy with big
teeth must say,
"Shut your mouth, Jack,
and quit slobbering,"
or "Zip up, Lawrence,
if I get horny you'll
be the last to know."

Snow must have brown
grass rising through it,
pastures must have
small daisies,
cows must have dark
flies on their backs
and around their eyes.

When the sun rises
you will have already
thrown a bale
of hay from the loft
and stepped
in some horseshit.
When you come into
the kitchen
everyone will know
where you've been.

A NOTE IN A VOICE

What the bird sings
is a memory of crows,
their black folding
and sailing across
hollows and hillsides.

This bird that has
no semblance of crow
except bird, singing
in the round of this
cove a remote song.

So her face has no
semblance of yours,
her way no semblance,
she who soars a
morning sky, open
and long ago.

A note in a voice,
forgotten
the large lies,
flapping off
to hollows and hillsides,
mind freed,
unwilling to control.

ROUND ROCK CREEK

1

Back to the meadow, back
to the crotch of hills
where the trapper
awakens in his lean-to,
rises to run his line.

Where tops of hickories
are the first to lose
color, their dull yellow
patching the warm comfort
of Round Rock Creek.

2

The mountain woman hulls
nuts in a pail, one
son at a last halves
the full kernels,

the other squats above
a stand of beeches,
his eyes narrow,
rifle poised and ready.

3

The farmer's easy movement
from barn mow to cattle,
splitting the dry oak,
fingers lean, knuckles
used and wrinkled.

The daughter carrying
wood from the sawbuck,
pushing the halting door
breasts rounded and firm
with fifteen years.

4

Hard hats gun their pickups
home, wooden steps to
trailers, tight kitchens,
dusk on the sealed roofs.

The careless beer and wine,
steel music, rows of lights
lining the hollow road
in Friday night invitation.

5

This picture, this escape
to Round Rock Creek,
a stranger once intrinsic,
now recreating time

and place, that graveled
life—real, yet never real,
a way then and forever
apart from the earth.

THE SWEETNESS OF FRENZY

At first you do not want
it. Though tempting, it comes
in an ugly disarray
of lines and ravels on your shirt.

You do not want it at
first because it speaks with
a strange voice that you feel
you would not want to know.

Awkward, limping, of no
worth outside the margin
of its own life, surely
it is flat and common.

And then when you take it
anyway, it was always
tempting, as you knew you
must, it draws the line taut,

runs, as you chase after,
master of confusion,
and you say, "Yes, there it
is and coming from there!"

Familiar now, though of
course you still cannot trust
it, must never trust it,
even when it seems to

know your name and strokes your
neck and whispers lowly
the sweetness of frenzy
stirred and of your success.

For you know that after,
always, comes the ending,
the waiting, the adding
and the striking out of

hope, watching it stray off,
distant and offering
no help, becoming its
egregious self again.

MAST

From the neighbor's yard to ours, squirrels
are bringing nuts to hide this morning,
digging holes in the lawn, burying
what mind says they can't find again.

However fascinating with their
magic tails, they dig like animals
everybody knows, dogs and sped-up
turtles, leaving most nuts half covered

to float up again in next month's
rain like coffins we heard of in last
spring's flood; here across the grass
like city rats come into the open

they have learned to live off humans,
in April eating lily bulbs,
pear blossoms, up trees cutting blooms
of nuts, spiting their own noses.

These are not the animals of children,
with ferret stealth seeding our pots
and yards as we sit defeated, raising
our cups in bemused tolerance.

We know they want no part of us,
rushing past November toward dens
of winter, storing and sleeping as if
happy to be rid of lives too
bountiful to evolve with theirs.

AN AUTUMN AFTERNOON

Eight members of my graduating
class are dead; a shove to the left
or right might have saved a couple
of them, but for the most part they
just ran out of genes; yesterday,
a wife of one of the eight, a teacher,
and I drove over to the clinic
near Clendenin; she was to have some
tests run and be mildly sedated.
We talked about everything (how
it was unusual for a class small
as ours to produce two preachers
and a missionary, plus half
a dozen nurses and teachers)
yet no one in particular,
and she was plenty worried.
She wouldn't know the results for
a week, and I was searching for some
words of hope, or comfort, when she
said she'd tried to love everyone
but now no one mattered. It was
an autumn afternoon and leaves
hurried along the road before us.
I tried to think how it must be
to love everyone, even harder
to think if no one mattered. As
I looked at her, then out the window
at the empty trees, I thought
the first thing to change if I were
God is to have her husband with her.

NIGHT DRAMA

The old ones cannot live without
tragedy: the abandoned cat
fed on the porch and fattened up
to die under the stranger's wheel,

the uncle camped on Lethe who
remembers well his lost driver's
license, two fists intended for
the face of the young examiner.

Old chests sobbing like children's,
faces accepting the pressure
of the weathered hand, feeling what
they thought they could not feel again.

Some thoughts they won't put on paper.
They play them in a dream and watch
all day the falling leaves fill up
the woods as if they were a bin.

They can live with pain, eye missing,
withered arm, their own God who has
taken their son, but the old ones
cannot live without tragedy.

FRIDAYS FAR AWAY AS HEAVEN

Monday, after two days off, they
unmuffle their loud trucks and drive
to plants, mills, garages, other
people's houses to unstop toilets
and put washers on their feet again.

Except in faces of relief,
they don't see themselves as saviors,
Fridays far away as heaven,
stepping outside the stench and grease
to dial a failed child or marriage.

Back inside, trained to be polite,
they underplay disaster, drop
our heat with steady hands, solder
pipes, and for cycles not yet right
order parts to be here Thursday.

Who they are or want to be at
night, they leave their tracks behind for
us to wonder at, the small joy
and grief that make a day or life,
a hand or voice to gloze the dark.

Weekends, we shut them off again,
having our stories topped by other
horrors, outraged and nodding that
prices shouldn't be the way they are.

On Monday morning we're customers
once more, trucks and tools rattling in
our drives, up early, opening doors
to greet them with our downcast smiles.

THE WORKMAN

". . . more fathers than sons themselves now."
—Donald Justice

The years are gradual as son
changes into father, long after
his own son pushes the homemade
truck on the birthday floor,

just before his own father sits
and dozes on a chair he has
all his life avoided, grandfather
who has lost his grip on wrenches.

The years between, to come, limbo
years of girls in green dresses
waving goodbye, rifles left in
cases, clothes that do not dazzle.

Riding the girder higher each
summer, straddling the beam of
a thousand lunches, patient with
young climbers, the artless foremen.

The view wider, the horizon
different, tame animal
that has treed him, no courage
now for jumping, too gray to fall.

EULOGY FOR BEN T. JOHNSON

Looking back on it, he did not
know what he might have changed,
the usual accidents bringing
him here to the ordinary.

There was corn to be planted so
he planted it, there was wood
to be chopped so he chopped it:
not just talking but getting done.

And if surely done himself, still
focused, the tree line outside
the window marching up the rising
field like soldiers disappearing.

Looking back on it, he saw the wind
taking him a direction
he would not go in repetition,
nor repeating go that way again.

Trees climbed the field, wind took the seeds
to ground that would accept them. Let
that change, how they faded into
the land, be his memorial.

NEAR BECKLEY

For a week now he has
not started his truck, back
and forth in a cold month
from barn to house, causing
her to say he might at
least go to the store and loaf.

There is no word again
today and as they sit
they wonder if what
the correspondent on
TV said was true: some
do not want to come back.

Her cousin's boy had been
killed outright and when they
brought the flagged box
into the church she got no
farther in her thoughts than
the shine on the soldier's boots.

She thought now about her
own boy's shoes and how each
morning after breakfast
and before the bus, he
shined them between his knees
and held them to the light.

She cannot remember
what she wanted for him then
or if she can she has
put it with old pieces
she used to save for quilts
on some forgotten shelf.

And what Webb thought, well
what man wasn't he like,
switching stations on and off
and talking gruff, wondering
if what the missing wished
is what those wishing do.

LETTER: AN ODE

*found among the papers of a certain
Rupert Fireash, address withheld*

Here at the bottom of the hill
I've found a rock, sort of a stone
bench, really, to write this letter
to you, not a friend or lover.

To ask how the weather is up
there, though you probably know that
by weather I don't mean weather
at all but how it is up there.

To ask how the kids are doing,
though as far as I know you didn't
marry, though you could have I don't
know, just trying for some answer.

If it was Mr. Right, I don't want
to know, I suppose; you could lie
and say that after me things were
never again the same somehow.

You could say at first you wanted
to die, that in every autumn
change you saw my face, that every
leaf brought a whisper with my voice.

Pardon that last; I'll strike it out.
I know you were never one to
put up with silly talk like that
as I was never one myself.

I could lie, too, and say that I'm
writing this letter from all of
us down here, but it's been too long
ago and pride is not worth that.

Well, I don't know if this will get
an answer; I haven't said much
about myself, though everybody
knows *I* is the one we write about.

Talk about weather, kids if you
have them, the way the wind blows
there in winter, the time you put that
scar upon your knee if you fell.

POEM FOUND IN AN OLD TRUNK

The dog cocks his leg
against the maple
sapling, then trots
past the cellar and
goes out the gate
toward the orchard.

The sun is white
through the fog as
I harness the horses
to mow between
the apple trees.

I hear the mail truck
change gears as it climbs
toward the post office
in Beech Valley.

A morning rising in
light the same as any
other these seven years.

She has moved away.

THE OTHER PLACE

The frosting of snow above
the thawing bank was
splattered with red mud from
the road where the truck passed.

When we reached the house, rooms
were cold and a cat, returned
from the woods, rubbed its
back against the doorsill.

Brown corn rattled
the garden, and we spoke
of their tire-chasing dog
riding somewhere away.

Maybe we all felt
guilty, something someone
had or had not done—
no one moved in winter.

When day had turned to
sunny afternoon, we
had forgotten them,
coats off now and wind warm,

as they must have forgotten,
there, wherever they were going,
the cat someone did not call—
or, called, would not come.

DARK COATS

Bright as a red dress on
a drab street to the eye
he was once to the stopped
moment when she, as he,

saw others in a mist
of dark coats going
to and from work or at
Christmas time in and out

of shops alone trying
to find right presents in
a world that was not right,
someone close lost or gone.

Now he, as she, the one
gone, not a flash but bar
of cloud after the red
has gone from the sunset

before moonrise, after
the bird has disappeared
from the horizon, settled
in the pond's tall grass.

The one who hears the fly
before death, though he is
not dying, who on the trip
home (cause long ago

ended), watches from modern
windows the quiet hills
passing, fallen into
the colors that sleep there.

NAMELESS

What she wanted was a song
she liked to sing and hear
others sing, a simple song
with passion; that was
all she wanted, she said,

and we sat on the bank
of the creek as locusts
gave her whispered words
a chorus and night
listened with its tiny eyes.

We were not in love
or rather she was not
in love with us, as we sat
the slope of grass and she
rested her cheek on her knee.

Nameless, as I think of you,
I think of all the words
I've dragged across the night
sky and do not remember,

roads we have both walked
back to our rooms in our
one-centeredness, hills that
stand bare for lack of song.

Every night was large then,
you with your absent riders,
making them our sadness,
as we unknowingly sang
your simple song with passion.

ON READING A POEM BY . . . .

When you meet a person
for the first time and like him
and don't wear your senses
out with familiarity, you remember
the feeling his name suggests.

Years later when you run across
the name again, maybe
in the newspaper or at a funeral,
you have the sense of tasting
a candy bar you had once as a kid

or the ease you have with a hand
on your shoulder, though he was never
a friend, just something better,
something untarnished by ocean,
unworn like the backbone of a hill.

So seeing your name today,
that you are a she doesn't matter,
I know the kind of audience one
must get meeting you at dinner
or having a drink in a cloudy bar.

That we won't meet is not bad,
surely better, not the fizzle of
appointment, but the spurt of match
that smoothly catches and lingers
awhile before you blow it out.

TODAY'S DATE

Seeing her at dusk sitting on
the porch banister smoking, he
walks up and down the road until
she notices, orders him over,
"Okay, dipshit, what do you want?"

We all know what will come of this:
they'll kiss, grow bolder, get married,
have two smartass kids, get older
and learn to hate each other.

That she'll switch from Lucky Strikes
to Virginia Slims will not change
her story, nor will the six o'clock
news, announcing future wars far
different from theirs, alter his.

And when they die, which they will in
accord with no one's protestation,
few will notice the calendar
that perhaps reads January 17, 2061.

Not quite off—they have their lives yet
before departure—they'll disregard
the things that merely matter,
their marvelous hands and speech,
her words that they'll forget, "Go home,
dickhead; there's nothing here for you."

KICK THE TIRE

It's useless to tell the dog
he can't catch the car by the tire;
he can't learn by words, just as we
can't be taught by words the alikeness
of our dog or child's magnificence.

Once or twice in history
someone or something has been
magnificent and maybe changed
a river or the way we act toward
others or the way we wear our hats.

Just as this fall is not the shortest
we have ever seen or last spring
the longest, we see little born
or dying that is not ordinary,
as our own faces are ordinary.

That they are rowels us to any
exaggeration of our own. We
don't know why the dog chases
the tire, the car pays no mind,
or why what we say about it
is so round and rubbery the same.

A NEIGHBORHOOD DOG

The dog yips as I halfheartedly
throw a pine cone to chase him
from the yard. When he reaches the spot
where there ought to be a fence,

he stops to stare. When I turn to
whatever job he has no interest in,
he turns too to the rabbit spoor
left last night in a nearby field.

It is a game we have played often
through the years, I to let him know
he is not my dog and he to assure
me he wouldn't be if I wanted him.

I don't know why he barks, what he
wants, I who like dogs well enough
outside my yard, as he is friendly
enough to those inside his own.

Grown older but no closer since
we met, dispute now diminished
to half growls, one might have killed
the other once were we that kind.

THE DUMPSTERS

Down at the dumpsters two dogs
have been let off. My neighbor
took one and someone shot
the other with a twenty-two.

That's the way it is there:
people either leaving off
or picking up, except for
shadows that creep in at dusk.

Besides the abandoned animals
it is the garbage people
who get the most attention,
not the men in trucks

but the unshaven or unshaped
ones in blue-faded cars
with windows halfway up,
bumpers masked with slogans.

Carrying sticks, they poke
the bulging bags as if they
are the bellies of the dead,
giving up their jewels and stench.

When we drive up, they keep
their booty close at hand;
clothed against filth and insult,
they move as if alone.

But when they speak, they are us:
"Amazing what people waste,"
"Perfectly good chair," "Government's
got their nose in everything."

When we drive off, they turn
to the bins, culling most of what
we've left, bones, mayonnaise
jars, a doll's rubber hand.

ANCESTRAL

Memory is never true. More
like a dream, the way we put
the extras in to round it out,
to give it story, to show the ones
we're telling to we may be worthy.

They know the lie, want it, so when
their turn comes round they can lean back
in demivolting fury or else
close in, shoulders together, to make
us sigh or yes our heads or stare.

It is the fiction now that pays,
the link that takes us back to the need
for warmth in groups, men's need for women,
women's need for men, women's
for women, the child's need for age.

Even if it is truer when we're
alone, when we drop the stone to
the bottom of the lake and go
diving there among light and shadows
for icons we need to right our lives,

it is still fancy. Yet it costs
us nothing, taking us near the ones
and things that are gone from our lives
forever save for this law that can
be broken, this gift from those lost times.

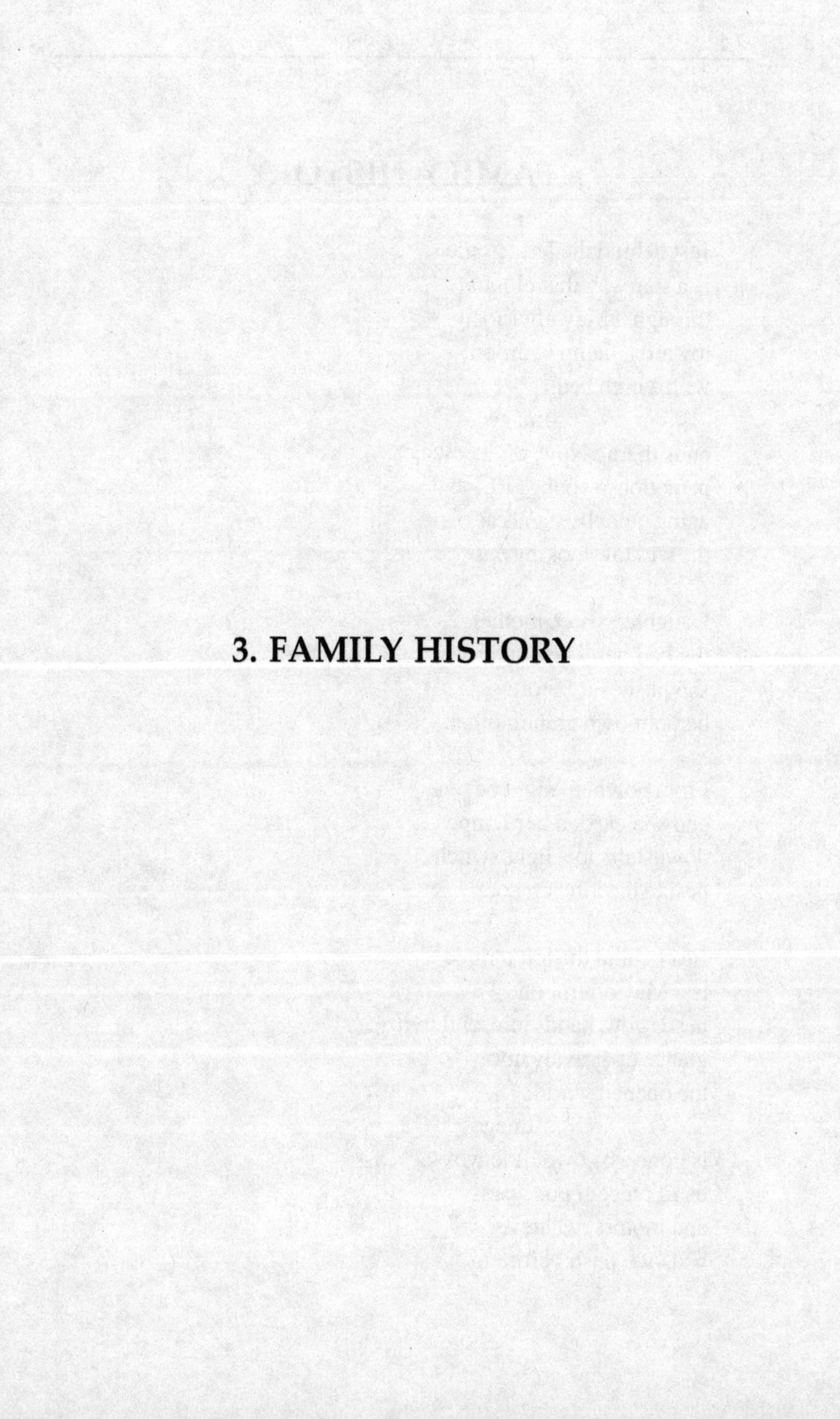

3. FAMILY HISTORY

FAMILY HISTORY

Just behind the left temple
is a stairway that climbs
through a May afternoon
toward a damp bedroom
with a high bed.
                    Image
ends there. Now, on its own,
in motion, a young girl,
aging quickly, stands at
the window looking out.

Daughter, sister, mother,
the bed her wheelbarrow,
she pushes it before
her, our own grandmother.

From nowhere night began
and she carried her lamp
downstairs to a light switch
beside the kitchen door.

Just behind the left temple
is a May afternoon,
heads bow, hands join, children
glance up gravely into
the opened world.
                    Image
is gone. Its own, it leaves
us to redeem our deeds
and motors, whatever
beds we push before us.

GRANDMOTHER

Helping with arguments
when he had to
Grandfather sat the porch
mostly,

shaving the tobacco plug,
chewing sparing
but regular.

He let Grandmother
do the work,
since she would,
Somebody has to,
Grandfather saying,
All right, Mother.

Because she always
stayed on the right
of things,
from saving the cow
not calf
when it breeched,
One milker is worth
three little bulls,
to correcting
the fourteen-cent mistake
on the store bill.

Except for once

when Grandfather
lost the big argument
she, Spare no cost,
bought the finest blue
coffin in the storeroom,

and standing beside him
on her own grave
finger down said,
That man all his life
walked, let him,
God grab his soul,
ride to Heaven
on golden wheels.

SURE TONES

We yell at the old ones
and when they don't understand
they pretend, holding
conversations with ghosts,

giving impossible answers,
changing the topic to
two years ago last winter
when the subject is zinnias.

At first we yell louder
but then unsettled by
the oh in their voices
our impatience causes,

we grow suspect of sound.
What we wish for most is
not their hearing back; they
can have that, even if

they never get quite used
to the batteries whistling,
soccer games in their head.
No, what we want back is

the Sunday afternoons
when they yelled at us at
the falls, the dog we could
not have, tones that were sure.

Lost now, we sit on porches
with them trying to make
them hear, trying to hear
ourselves not just those gone

voices but the perfect
blend that is not denial
or telling, that music
by which we speak and hear.

NOMENCLATURE

The trouble with my dad
and me was nomenclature:
he'd ask for a Crescent
and I'd bring a box end
forever the wrong size;

he'd ask for a hole saw,
I'd bring a drill bit,
ball-peen, a tack hammer;
a saw horse, I'd dream
a ticket to the fair.

Searching, I could out-swear
him, kicking the useless
toolbox aside, muttering
with the worst of him about
a quick road out of town.

Now it's similes for
metaphors, synecdoche
for metonymy, images
that show by the dead tree
there're no pears left to prize.

He made a wagon for us
once. Here, he said and went
inside. It rode all right.
All I wanted, one time, was
wasted breath, one tired lie.

BRIGHTEST, REDDEST APPLES

What bothers him most, at least
today, is the quick way things change:
yesterday his gang was the brightest,
reddest apples on the tree, faces

in tight shot needing but a splash
of water, his hands so smoothly
masculine they seemed just
modeled from a chapel ceiling;

now, it's laughs behind his back as
he comes home by way of drugstore
from the doctor's office to study
a box he's taken from his pocket.

What bothers him today is that
yesterday when recess ended,
he knew a bell would ring classes
tomorrow, learning nothing from

the death of relatives, as the sun
learns nothing from its faded neighbors,
unable to believe in his
radiance absent from the earth.

MR STEVENS

He put on his checkered
shirt, his khaki pants,
crooked a gun in his arm,
and guarded his own farm.

Mr Stevens is not in,
he would say or
Mr Stevens is a busy man
and cannot be disturbed.
Come back tomorrow maybe.

Once one of our cousins
went to visit. He said,
But you are Mr Stevens.
Your name is Henry. I am
Cousin Frank. I have come
to borrow a whiffletree.

You are a goddamn spy,
Henry said. Mr Stevens
warned me about spies.
Then he shot an inch
above Cousin Frank's head
and blew his hat off.

Once the Widow Kelly came
to call. She shook the
chain on his gate and said,
See here, Henry, see here.

Henry hurried to the gate.
Mr Stevens sees no whores,
he said, and reached between
the bars and tore at
the Widow Kelly's cleavage.

One day Mr Stevens died.
Henry dressed him in his
shirt and khaki pants and
buried him behind the barn.

He became very friendly.
He loaned Cousin Frank
a whiffletree and made
love with the Widow Kelly.

But sometimes he wanted
to dig up Mr Stevens. He
wanted to choke him and
spit in his face. Sometimes
he wanted to kill him
and take back his clothes.

BUT ITS OWN

Over the ground I walk
on which he walked and now
lies under, I have walked
with my children and wife,
mother and grandmother,
father and grandfather.

A hill that overlooks
houses of those that all
hours might have stood in yards,
on porches, and seen where
they too, barring nothing,
would lie down separately.

The day is any day,
but its own, crows quiet
in the wooded hollows
once fields for the houses
with yards and porches, earth
in no way singular.

Seeds that blew, took root, bore
lie under wind above
the ground on which I walk,
over which he walked tall
as a poplar, too long
ago now for grieving.

MOTHER'S VOICES

Yesterday there was a voice;
today there is none. That's the way
it is when you lose the sound of
someone who's been always in your ear.

You heard the ring and you took it,
all those years of distinguishing
one tone from another, then
filtering out the hurt not meant

to last longer than the moment;
the it's all right you said later,
the tear that came too easily
dried after years of subtle wear.

It will not awake for breakfast
to say the sun they promised might
just come today, hoping eaves held
until that fellow came to fix them.

Today is sunny; sound carries well
out of the west where a breeze brings
the soft talk of neighbors telling
the postponement of pressing repair.

But voice is not there—the way
it told the clock, the obits in
the paper, the natural way
it broke between dishes and hands.

HOME PLACE

They claim the house where I was born
their home place and own it still, our
father selling it, moving to
town our widowed neighbor said, though
the ones who lived there, including
her, made up not a hundred names.

Even if less and less I live there
still—the sudden foggy mornings
when cattle move like ghosts around
the barn, the beetled afternoons—
they have the deed to rearrange
any memories as their own.

When we played together, they could
have it free since any toy given
away was still our own, a whim
that but a moment might reverse,
as the oak might reclaim in spring
the dazzle it had given to the fall.

Can two or even more families
have one home? It was not new when
we moved in. Perhaps memories
are best kept by the house itself
loaning us its boards and land to
hoard our secrets, earning our
courtesy which we in turn give them.

SANDY SCHROEDER, BRIDE

The birds were especially noisy
the spring before you died, rain
plentiful, dogwoods white and pink
aligning every street and drive.

Then the summer you were twenty-
six and you stood, white-brimmed hat,
pregnant, on the grass before
your house to have your picture made.

You said life was just beginning
and pushed your hands along your front
of dress and laughed and then, a child,
ran to pose beside the tulip garden.

That fall in Brohard, West Virginia,
leaves came down in baskets; nights held
clear and frost bit gently kernels
of hickories and black walnuts.

The fall this year is like that fall.
Walking, I am reminded of a day
of falling leaves when your death
mattered to everyone I knew.

At twenty-six no one's life is
just beginning. The shutter snaps
and lies, our smiles reversed in that
darkness between the blush and film.

AUNT PHYLLIS

No one thought of Aunt Phyllis
as anything more than a nosy
relative searching for night scraps.
She could take the smell straight
out of morning coffee, rumoring
red spots into breakfast
eggs, putting the cry back
into milk spilled, quitting
a world fast quitting her.

Then when worst was surely
over, she burst onto the end
of Christmas Eve, the button
and hole not matching on her
sweater, to say Grandmother
had once taken a hired man
as lover, so who knew which
of us might be a bastard or, just
as bad, sitting next to one.

If every life needs form, she
was the change that reels us
together when we stand outside
facing a north wind with
a burned-out house behind us,
or the change we need when
after months of evacuation, we
return to an overcast sky that
promises more desperate weather.

JOE AND UNCLE JESSE

"I quit," he said,
"just quit.
Happen you find
enough air
left in the tires
of that old '87 Plymouth,
have her!
But I'm through."

What else he said
I'm damned
if I remember;
he just stepped
off the store porch,
walked a half-mile
down the road
to Haverstraw's,
beat the whole field
at shuffle board,
and laid down and died.
In style, by God.

TREADING TIME

for Kendall

Where the hickories have
been cut for the new road
we gather firewood. We
remember the old way.

The gas line runs under
the meter house and we
watch the many needles,
fast, slow, some not moving.

The wind in the old oaks
takes us away from each
other and you, staring,
see things I never saw.

And I see trees empty
of their leaves, at first cold,
December, then spring when
buds begin to sharpen.

You tell me that the drought
this year brought no mast
for the animals; you say
that that is nothing new.

We throw the wood over
the fender of the truck
and I notice the gray
beginning in your hair.

At the house you bring Scotch
in a brandy glass. You say
your daughter just finished
college. I say, mine too.

THE GARDEN

In a tin shed my brother
puts out a battery-run
radio to keep deer
out of his sweet corn.

We walk down to the garden
at night and listen
to the hidden ghosts
singing to each other.

Though the voices seem
lower when we return
the next morning,
they surprise us still.

Raccoons have ravaged
the field: leaves shredded,
tassels broken, the white
of canvas gloves.

Well, that worked,
he says, switching off
the radio, tearing
foil from the antenna.

We parade down rows, looking
at the half-eaten ears,
obscenities flying from
his mouth like ticker tape.

I thought those damned
things were extinct,
he says, not meaning it,
kicking at clods.

Then, looking away from
each other, past animals,
the blue hills, we laugh like
brothers, like West Virginians.

SMITTYS

The ordinary man sat at a table
in the darkness. Not that he didn't
like the music, not that he didn't
like the red dancers in the light.

The truth is he liked them very much;
he sat in his dark shoes and kept
time with his fingers on his glass.
He smiled and nodded approval.

The ordinary man didn't mind
the green hair of the dancers, the thin
legs and deep skirts, the creased pants
in limbo below the simple bar.

It was a dark table where he sat.
He smiled and drummed his fingers,
nodding approval, as if he
didn't care what part he was of the show.

THE COLOR OF THE SKY

The two of us were just
drifting along, about the same
age, I perhaps a year or two
older, in a green metal boat
we had borrowed from someone,
maybe a friend of his uncle,

the light anchor bumping
the bottom of the pond, our lines
trailing after, the wind and sky
unnoticeable when he said,
I'm going to join up. Join what?
I said. He said, The Marines.

Until then, we knew pretty much
everything about each other,
girlfriends, scars, all the particulars
of going in one direction
that brought us to this tug of boat
with anchor suddenly fastened.

I don't recall much after,
a uniform maybe, buttons
brighter than the sun, speech
full of initials, hearing from
others about camps, promotions,
marriage to a girl in Japan.

The second part of everything began
then, though the first seems longer,
pirates of time, mavericks on water
who drifted out too many years
for docking, singularly afloat
in our strangely different lives.

GAY

When you hold his hand
I try to understand
by thinking of
heterosexual love,

her hand in mine,
say, or watching highway
and mountains through
the windshield all day long,

suddenly turning
and catching her watching
face that, once caught,
smiles, wanting nothing else.

I do not know
if I am close; I don't
know what to ask,
how not to be embarrassed.

Asking, father
to his son, I know that,
a son myself,
words are bricks in your mouth

and offer this:
Is a date the way I felt
in high school asking
Vicki to the dance?

to be stood up,
the way I feel here, not
knowing what I've
done wrong or what I lack,

yet wanting still
another chance to prove
I am worthy
of trust and confidence?

Tonight in our
secret worlds I strive to
learn something right,
to be the man behind

you when you're dressed,
to help you with your ties,
to let you live
with love I cannot know.

STAYING

The house a party of motion,
camp, college, marriage—all the same:
something in a drawer almost
left behind, the double-checked closet.

No time yet for sidelong glances
or hang-down eyes, bodies scuffling,
a sudden cry at not much time,
flush of toilet, trunk lid slammed.

Standing like two birds we watch the
car back out the drive, a fluttering
hand between boxes that tilt, then
jostle and settle for the ride.

Daughter, daughter, have we prepared
you half so well for days ahead,
when clothes, lockets are forgotten,
when dark days and nights greet you with

surprises not taught here, and you
find a woman inside leaving
behind the girl you thought you were
because we thought you were that girl?

Like two birds we return to the branch
of our own lives, wondering if
we are lucky not to be true birds,
perched above nests emptied every year.

4. EDGES OF ROADS

BACK ROAD TO CHARLESTON

The calf, probably six
months old, stands at the edge
of the road ready to bolt.
I slow the car willing
to follow any lead,

then pass slowly, watching
it wobble in glass to
the center line and stand
again, seeing what calves
see, failed in direction.

I top the slow hill full
of options: try to find
its owner, find someone
who might find its owner,
get out and flag others.

And then, like God, do none
of these things, my wife's plane
due in Charleston,
morning sky suddenly
dark with our own dangers.

How right it would be to
have answers, smile down on
all highways and runways,
sure, shifting on without
the guilt of excuses.

I try the radio for
weather, static snapping,
and see the calf in the rain
that is coming, raising
its head, dripping, bawling.

COAL FORK

The hollow as wet and sour
as a wrung dishcloth, smoke
that won't go up, red mud
from boots on the back steps.

"Where are the car keys, Myrt?"
"You kids stay out of that
garden—it's too wet." Dog
raining the baby awake.

The new girl well stacked
at the Kwik Sack only
a dirty joke, gestures—
his kind of infidelity.

Not impressed by magazine
models, her blouse half out,
she talks back, not to be
confused with the soap set.

"You had them last." Mock
rebuff and grab of ass,
his head out the window
looking back, driving off.

Wide-angled, gnat on a road
along a shallow creek,
a line of houses, pride
not even they believe.

STRAIGHT CREEK

They have taken the bell
from the steeple and hung
it from a yoke between
two posts before the church.

The hillside field beside
it where horses galloped
once and boys caught and rode
them belongs to the night.

Though the air is dry and leaves
come down in bursts, it is
still summer, the long drought
unaffected by the small rain.

What the church meant beyond
its symbol to this town
I don't know, though I too
leaned my head in its pews

once and listened to the rough
words of elders, studying
the calligraphy in
hymnals and Betty Brown.

I do not know what it
is I could not learn, what
if it ever drifted down
passed through my hands like wind.

The bell is out of the steeple
now. Palpable as that bell,
surely, to them, cleansing
as the smile of Betty Brown.

COUNTRY CHURCH

She recalls,
walking up the aisle,
how he pushed
his thick life
into her Saturday night

and knows
if invitations had been
granted for this affair
none would have been
sealed for her,

but had he not
been hers
a back seat wide?
and was not the proof
of his young years
hard beneath the belly
of her dress?

Whose right then
if not hers
to raise the net
and kiss
the dead mouth
that once said enough
to get her
where she was?

Turning down the aisle,
every eye askance,
she knows the dress
cannot hide what
she was to him:

but feeling the sun
on her face
when she walks
through the gravel
to her car,

she names a name,
not sanctioned here,
to be his
when life breaks
like a plant
from the grave.

HUGHES RIVER

As river meets the bend
there is a small
clearing where last night
someone's campfire burned.

The spot is clean except
for a circle of stones
around black cinders, ash
like flux for soldering.

Not fishermen: no bait
remains or nest of line;
no boot tracks or hole props,
no lost hooks, no odor.

Nor lovers, grass upright,
absence of cans, paper,
bottles, as if sun, air
hold no notion of love.

Someone spent with life, its
brood and entanglements,
not knowing moon's quarters
or the color of skies.

A matchbox left over,
drawer open, faded cover,
tilted there between
the highway and the fire.

MACFARLAN BRIDGE

The Macfarlan bridge is
down, cables cut, wooden
floor and rusty girders
hauled away in trucks.

The sides of the new bridge,
cement white, no steel rod
showing, rise and block
the view of the river.

As a child, asleep at
night behind my father's
driving, I woke to boards
rattling, the signal

that the trip from town was
over. Later, friends
and I walked to the river
and climbed, against parents'

wishes, the taut wires
to the top braces. No one
thought of falling then,
and no one did, for water

was a flowing away
from grown-up things to birds
that flew and could not fall
or fish that never drowned.

It is the permanence
of this bridge now, as I
stop today and look over:
no careless swaying, the dark

water claiming, drawing
my weight forward until
in panic I push away
and turn against falling.

In my car I drive away
trembling, that man back there,
gaunt, consenting, adult
in his body-breaking fall.

THE KANAWHA

I

Underbrush has covered the car
someone died in; only when frost has
stripped trees to brittle selves does
chrome betray its final skidding.

Old, river below, let it rust,
the owner long hidden under
his ton of earth, attendants who
cared so much then used to their loss.

II

In a trailer a mile beyond
the bend of river, hidden by
a bluff, a Viet Nam POW
drinks tea on his make-shift porch

and remembers eating rats when
he could catch them, quiet sidling
and furtive squeaking, their eyes
shining like dog tags in the dark.

III

Bargemen retell the Indian
legend of lovers from opposing
tribes forbidden to marry,
how they leapt, hands together, from

an eastern cliff and on spring nights
their cries falling on Charleston,
their hair catching the light, holding
them forever an evening star.

IV
Often when the water reflects
the moon, masked scavengers of night
escape the hounds to crack mussels
on the rocks and deer, returned again,

come down to drink, water lapping
the banks, frightened when fishermen
scrape a paddle on their boat, drifting
the far shore, running their trotline.

V
Winter, water on its secret
passage below ice that seldom
ventures far from shore, bright between
the stripped hollows and hills.

It is the light betrays, dancing
off whatever reflects it, this old
Kanawha, frenzied beginning,
its mystery familiar and tame.

THEY MADE THE BEST RED WHISKEY
IN WIRT COUNTY

Out the dirt road past
the telephone relay
tower, fog and mud mock
the windshield wipers.

They stop and get out,
talking about getting more
beer, listening to the tall
oaks drip and urinating
into the water.

Around them the frightened eyes
that might be watching
have turned inward, and one
says they just as well have
stopped at the guard station.

They talk of shooting some
quickness into the ridges,
challenging the slick roads
toward Dever's Fork,
getting more beer.

In Parkersburg, two brothers
are sitting before a rainy
window playing poker; they
do not hear the passing traffic.
They would kill to win.

ROMEY DAVIS

A bare tree stands against
the sky on a hilltop
a half mile from the house.
It is night and winter.
All afternoon it snowed,
but now the moon invites
night animals to come
from their dens and feed.
A star rises in the tree.

In the house a man is dead.
Relatives stoke the fire
and women talk quietly.
None say but would agree
the right amount of mourning
for one too old to live.

But night will miss this
man, who hunted foxes
and frightened owls, who set
steel traps in streams, who
reminded nature what it is.

He would not describe himself
this way, the star this way,
the moon, the snow, the tree.
He did not think that he
should die. No one views
a winter scene the same.

MONA RICHARDS, RT. 4

September, the smell of death
hides in the dry fields
and leaves are gilded
by the hanging air drifting
from the county road.

The garden has threaded to
weeds and in the pine
above the creek a crow
gives three shrill calls.

When was there a better month
for the letter that lies
unopened on the table
in the hall, the wrinkled
envelope, the barely
legible scrawl, when was
there a better year
for it to come too late.

The contents who can guess:
a cold story too tired to tell
about loneliness and love
and hate, but mostly about
handwriting that is old.

I had thought of moving
to town this fall. Now
I will go. Lord knows
the seasons this place has
lived off my false hope.

Yes, I will go. Strange
color tints the hickories
this year and my life seems
all unreal—as if never lived
at all, static and rooted,
as if a hickory tree whose
leaves could never fall.

SONATA

The state trooper snaps his fingers
and says, Just like that. One minute
you're driving along enjoying
John Denver and the next, snapping
his fingers again, it's no man's land.
How a glass one second past full
of your favorite drink lies shattered
on the deck of a swimming pool.

Effective seminar.

A cross on some highway
for a little while marks the spot
of the accident, a ghostless grave.
In dead grass along the interstate
the overturned tanker killed,
dandelions and timothy
have seeded, making a comeback.

Mother Grim, may I go swim?
Oh, yes my darling daughter.
Just hang your clothes on a hickory limb,
but don't go near the water.

SPENCER HIGH SCHOOL

Fall comes again, but for
those going back to school
it is the beginning
of the year.
              Bus drivers
sit before the vacant
faces that watch down as
we follow them in our cars.

We remember our first
terms, mothers wetting down
our hair with their hands, then
our own children;
                  now their
children squirm in their new
shirts and dresses, and we
slow to other roads.

Growing up was something
others did then, older
brothers, with no time for
us, catching the car keys,

the blond girl down the street
with a crush on silly
Frank, confiding in us
because we could be trusted.

How short a time we live,
we say, yet except for
sudden moments when hearts
seem to falter,
                    when legs
are air and we lean on
workbenches or the kitchen
table, our minds deny.

We know the lie, just as
we knew then that we would
catch the keys of older
brothers;
              meanwhile we turn
our corner, faces in
the windows solemn still
as they watch us out of sight.

SMOKE

In the air the smell of
smoke so strong the taste
of bacon touches the tongue
and teases the mind.

It is autumn and a time
for walking before first
snow floods the air and soots
branches and hillside cliffs.

This morning, coming down
a draw, in a thicket just
below the road, I freed
a deer, his antlers caught

in heavy vines, front legs
down, his eyes almost tame
with struggle. In a month
he will likely go down

again, his slick coat stained,
his antlers trophy for some
hunter, but today he
forgives the scent of man.

Keats was right to say fall
has its song, hickory smoke,
the buck by now stripping
saplings: this season, when

sky is bluest and hills
seem taller, when Death
is only a jester
behind his motley hood.

WEST VIRGINIA OIL

The commotion
and twenty-four hour
drilling is over,
left only the toy
rocking of
a broken horse
at the feeding tank.

The doe by the creek
does not drink the water;
it is salt
coming in a trickle
down the runnel
from the overspill
of the holding pit.

At night, all quiet
except cicadas and owls
under a heavy moon
in summer,
wind and blowing snow
covering the tracks
of winter.

Somewhere, rooms are
heated with the laughter
of cut diamonds,
rooms heated
by the mechanic

in an oily chair
cleaning his rifle.

Up, down the toy horse,
flooding the lines,
a rich day in autumn,
up the far hillside
the doe drinking, the spring
sweet as if from
some found paradise.

COMING FROM THERE

An orange, a round
light rolling the road's
air, the boy stepped aside
and watched it miss
the turn and explode
against the hillside.

Years he knew about
the tracking, but now
artillery? What madness
could he pretend to explain
this madness? what excuse
to excuse the nearness?

Should he leave the road
at last, take to hills
and underbrush, stumble
blindly down any thicket,
hoping to meet the
road again by accident?

The road, the black road
he thought would lead
to safety (who told
him so in strictest
confidence long ago?),
strewn always with mines.

Now he could pretend no
longer: so: no madness,
no excuses; this darkness
admitted: the way itself
salvation, a road with
no end, coming from there.